Jessica Bordeleau

Abundant Grace

A Gift from God

Devotional Prayer Journal

The vision of CTA is
to see Christians highly effective
in their ministry so that Christ's Kingdom
is strengthened and expanded.

A Gift from God

Jessica Bordeleau

Copyright © 2019 CTA, Inc.
1625 Larkin Williams Rd.
Fenton, MO 63026
www.CTAinc.com

Printed in Thailand
ISBN: 978-1-947699-11-3

Abundant Grace

Some words are always welcome . . .

I kept your supper warm.

Have a chocolate?

We're almost home.

I love you!

Perhaps the sweetest, most welcome word of all, though, is the word *grace*. When you live in the grace of God, the crushing load of sin and its guilt can fall off your back. Shame has no place in your heart. You can stop trying to earn God's love through your good deeds. You can lay down the overwhelming pressure to achieve.

The grace of God sets you free to be alive and active in your Christian faith—without fear. Knowing God's good and gracious will to give you an eternal future in Christ outweighs every burden you bear and strengthens you to carry those burdens with good cheer.

When you are united with Christ through faith, the abundant grace of God defines your past, present, and future! The Bible assures us:

For all have sinned and fall short of the glory of God, and are justified by his grace as a gift, through the redemption that is in Christ Jesus.

Romans 3:23–24

This prayer journal is designed to comfort, strengthen, and challenge you to recognize the daily significance of God's grace in your life. May the Lord open your eyes and heart to his amazing grace!

>Grace, grace, God's grace,
>Grace that will pardon and cleanse within;
>Grace, grace, God's grace,
>Grace that is greater than all our sin!

Julia H. Johnston, 1911

For from his fullness we have all received,
grace upon grace.

John 1:16

God doesn't draw his grace from a limited supply; his storehouse is full and overflowing. His mercy and forgiveness never run out. Because of Jesus, God pours his grace and forgiveness into your life constantly, day after day. Write a prayer of thanks for the abundant grace God continually gives!

Take a full pitcher of water and a glass to your kitchen sink. As you pour the entire pitcher of water into the glass and watch it spill over the rim, be reminded of how God's forgiveness overflows for you and for those around you.

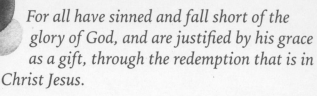

For all have sinned and fall short of the glory of God, and are justified by his grace as a gift, through the redemption that is in Christ Jesus.

Romans 3:23–24

As a child you may have been told that "Santa brings presents only to good little girls." If that were true, there would be a lot of disappointed children on Christmas morning! If imperfect earthly parents give good gifts to their children, imagine how much more your *perfect* heavenly Father wants to bless you with his own good gifts! God's grace is a free gift and it has your name on it! How does that realization impact your understanding of God's love for you?

Tangible Grace

Find a gift tag and write "ABUNDANT GRACE from: Your heavenly Father, to: _____". Write your name in the blank. If you don't have a gift tag, make one. Use the tag as a bookmark in your Bible this week.

Through [our Lord Jesus Christ] we have also obtained access by faith into this grace in which we stand, and we rejoice in hope of the glory of God.

Romans 5:2

God's grace gives you hope and a reason to rejoice. In Christ you have the sure and certain hope that the eternal life you enjoy now will continue on forever in heaven. That truth opens up a new perspective on life's hardships. What are you struggling with today? How does your hope in Christ equip you to stand up to those challenges?

Tangible Grace

Write "I stand on God's grace!" on a piece of paper and tape it to your bathroom mirror. Each time you see it, remember that no matter what you face today, your future in heaven is secure.

Grace to you and peace from God our Father and the Lord Jesus Christ.

In him we have redemption through his blood, the forgiveness of our trespasses, according to the riches of his grace, which he lavished upon us.

Ephesians 1:2, 7–8

Write the letters *G-R-A-C-E* vertically down this page. Then write these words beside each letter: **G**od's **R**iches **A**t **C**hrist's **E**xpense. This acronym provides one common definition of grace. With his own blood, Jesus paid the debt of our sins. In exchange, we receive the lavish riches of grace. What are some of the spiritual riches God has given you?

_____

_____

_____

_____

_____

_____

_____

_____

_____

_____

_____

_____

_____

_____

_____

_____

_____

_____

_____

_____

_____

_____

_____

Tangible Grace

Invite a friend out for coffee or dessert and tell
her the bill is on you. Use this small example of
covering someone else's expense to remind
yourself of the amazing grace of Christ, who
covered your debt in full!

Three times I pleaded with the Lord about this, that it should leave me. But he said to me, "My grace is sufficient for you, for my power is made perfect in weakness."

2 Corinthians 12:8–9

We don't know which weakness the apostle Paul asked the Lord to remove in 2 Corinthians 12, but God's answer was clear. He didn't give Paul what he asked for; he gave him something better! He does the same for you. God doesn't promise to take away all your hardships, but he promises to be with you in them. His powerful love will sustain you through the darkest situations, when you are at your weakest. Describe a time when the Lord blessed you by giving you something that was better than what you prayed for.

Tangible Grace

Take a moment to read Isaiah 43:1–2.
Then thank the Lord for being with you
   through times of hardship, despite your
   weakness.

For you, O Lord, are good and forgiving, abounding in steadfast love to all who call upon you.

Psalm 86:5

God showed his abounding love to you by sending his Son, Jesus, to pay the price for your sins. His forgiveness is for you and he has plenty of it! No sin is too small. No sin is too big. No number of sins is too many for him to forgive. Confess your sins to him. You can trust his abundant mercy!

Tangible Grace

In the Lord's abundant forgiveness he washes you clean. As you shower today, think of how many drops of water are falling to wash you clean. Even if your hot water runs out, God's forgiveness never will!

But if it is by grace, it is no longer on the basis of works; otherwise grace would no longer be grace.

Romans 11:6

If you work for it, it's called a paycheck. If you don't deserve it, it's called grace. You don't deserve God's love, but you have it! As you pray today, thank your Lord Jesus for giving you what you could never earn on your own.

Tangible Grace

Is there someone in your life who doesn't
deserve your forgiveness? Give it anyway
and pray for him or her today.

God is our refuge and strength, a very present help in trouble. Therefore we will not fear though the earth gives way, though the mountains be moved into the heart of the sea.

Psalm 46:1–2

When it feels like your entire world is crashing down and your strength is gone, you can be assured that one thing will never change. God's love for you is rock solid, unmovable. Describe a time when the stability of God's love helped you stand firm in a difficult time.

_____
_____
_____
_____
_____
_____
_____
_____
_____
_____
_____
_____
_____
_____
_____
_____
_____
_____
_____
_____
_____

Tangible Grace

Find a picture of a mountain in a book or online.
Imagine the splash (the tsunami!) if that enormous
mass of rock were dropped into the ocean! Even when
you feel as though you've been hit by a tidal
wave, you can be certain that the Lord's grace
stands firm. He is your solid ground.

The LORD is near to the brokenhearted and saves the crushed in spirit.

Psalm 34:18

The hardships of life can break our hearts. The Lord promises to be near you even when you are crushed by grief. You are never alone! How has his presence brought comfort in your life?

Tangible Grace

Wear a bracelet today. Each time you see it or
feel it on your wrist, be reminded that the Lord
is present with you today and every day.

Let us then with confidence draw near to the throne of grace, that we may receive mercy and find grace to help in time of need.

Hebrews 4:16

Do you ever feel too unworthy or ashamed to approach God in prayer? The forgiveness that Jesus earned for you gives you total access to the throne of grace. Your heavenly Father invites and encourages you to speak with him. You can approach him with confidence! Describe the difference between being confident and being fearful. Then claim that confidence as your own!

Tangible Grace

Spend time in prayer today, confident that the
Lord invites you to come to him, hears your
every word, and longs to spend time
with you!

Let the wicked forsake his way, and the unrighteous man his thoughts; let him return to the LORD, that he may have compassion on him, and to our God, for he will abundantly pardon.

Isaiah 55:7

Abundant

pardon! That's what the Lord promises when you confess your sins to him, not just a little forgiveness to cover the small sins but enough forgiveness to wash away each and every sin—every one of them. Through Jesus we have complete, absolute, abundant pardon!

Tangible Grace

Check your cleaning supplies. Shake the soap bottles. Which one is fullest? As you do this, remember that because of Jesus, God's forgiveness for you will never run short.

There is no fear in love, but perfect love casts out fear. For fear has to do with punishment, and whoever fears has not been perfected in love.

1 John 4:18

God showed his perfect love to you by sending Jesus to live and die for you. Jesus took the punishment you deserved when he died on the cross. Fear of punishment need not stand in the way of your relationship with God anymore. Which of your fears can melt away in the assurance that Christ has earned peace for you?

Tangible Grace

Take an ice cube out of your freezer and hold it in
your hand under warm running water. As the ice
melts away, think of how your fear of God's
punishment melts away because of the
cross of Christ.

He saved us, not because of works done by us in righteousness, but according to his own mercy, by the washing of regeneration and renewal of the Holy Spirit, whom he poured out on us richly through Jesus Christ our Savior, so that being justified by his grace we might become heirs according to the hope of eternal life.

Titus 3:5–7

When someone dies, that person's heirs receive his possessions. No one earns an inheritance; it is given to anyone who is named in the will. By God's mercy and grace, you have been named an heir and you have received eternal life. Because of Christ Jesus, you can look forward to something fabulous! How can remembering your future impact your attitude today?

Tangible Grace

Open your calendar, chose a random
day next week, and insert these words:
"Because of Jesus, I have a fabulous future!"

But while he was still a long way off, his father saw him and felt compassion, and ran and embraced him and kissed him.

Luke 15:20

In the parable of the lost son, a young man runs away from home, only to find a life filled with misery. He returns home, planning to ask to work for his father as a slave. But before he can say a word, his father runs to him, hugs him, welcomes him home, and reinstates his full privileges as a member of the family. Put yourself in the story. How do you respond to undeserved love like that?

Tangible Grace

Who in your life could use a warm welcome?
Whether it's at a family gathering or a worship
service, show genuine acceptance to
someone who seems uncomfortable.

But God, being rich in mercy, because of the great love with which he loved us, even when we were dead in our trespasses, made us alive together with Christ—by grace you have been saved.

Ephesians 2:4–5

Have you ever seen a dead animal on the side of the road? It's awful! Yelling out the car window at such an animal will accomplish nothing. Likewise, before God gives us new life by faith in Jesus, we are spiritually dead—dead in sin. How does that comparison, together with the above passage from Ephesians 2, deepen your understanding of God's grace in Christ's cross?

Tangible Grace

I hope you don't see any dead animals on the side of the
road this week . . . but if you do, remember that you
were just as dead in your sin, but not anymore!
God has saved you by his grace and made
you alive in Christ Jesus!

For by grace you have been saved through faith. And this is not your own doing; it is the gift of God, not a result of works, so that no one may boast. For we are his workmanship, created in Christ Jesus for good works, which God prepared beforehand, that we should walk in them.

Ephesians 2:8–10

You aren't saved by your own good deeds, yet you are called to walk in righteousness. What difficult concepts to balance! Jesus earned salvation for you. He gives it to you by grace through faith in him. Your good deeds are a response to what he has already done for you. What kinds of service do you most enjoy doing in thankfulness for what God has already done for you?

Tangible Grace

Who in your life needs to see the love of Christ?
In grateful joy, plan a way to serve that person.

And God is able to make all grace abound to you, so that having all sufficiency in all things at all times, you may abound in every good work.

2 Corinthians 9:8

When my great-grandmother refused second helpings at the dinner table, she would say: "I've had sufficient, thank you." It was her polite way of saying she was full. God has filled you up with his love and forgiveness. That love nourishes your soul and equips you for action. Which act of service has God called you to do today?

Tangible Grace

As you eat dinner this evening, thank God for
both for the food on your plate and the spiritual
nourishment he gives you in his Word.

For you know the grace of our Lord Jesus Christ, that though he was rich, yet for your sake he became poor, so that you by his poverty might become rich.

2 Corinthians 8:9

When the batteries in your flashlight are dead, you exchange them with live batteries. That's a down-to-earth picture of what God has done for you in Christ. Jesus died the death *we* deserve, and in exchange we receive the reward of eternal life—life only *he* deserves. Life in exchange for death. How does thinking about that light up your day?

Tangible Grace

Check the batteries in your flashlight. Still working?
If not, exchange any dead battery you find with a
good one. Be reminded that God has given you
new life in Christ in exchange for the
death you deserve!

*For I am sure that neither death nor life,
nor angels nor rulers, nor things present
nor things to come, nor powers, nor height
nor depth, nor anything else in all
creation, will be able to separate us from
the love of God in Christ Jesus our Lord.*

Romans 8:38–39

Neither guilt over yesterday nor fears about tomorrow need shake your confidence in God's love for you. Today's struggles are real. They are difficult. But God's love for you is stronger. He put that love into action by sending his only Son for you. What worries are crowding into your mind today? Let Jesus take those cares, replacing them with confident hope.

Tangible Grace

Read Romans 8:38–39 out loud!

But I am like a green olive tree in the house of God. I trust in the steadfast love of God forever and ever, because you have done it. I will wait for your name, for it is good, in the presence of the godly.

Psalm 52:8–9

Some trees are small and spindly; others are mighty and majestic. In his grace the Lord enables you to thrive like a healthy tree. The spiritual fruits of peace, hope, and joy are evident and maturing in you because of what God has done for you in Christ. Write a prayer asking God to enable you to grow in faith and in fruit bearing as his Holy Spirit works in you.

Tangible Grace

Draw a picture of a big healthy tree. It doesn't matter if you are an artist or not, even a simple drawing will do. Under the tree write these words: "I am like a thriving tree. I will praise God for what he has done!"

I am he who blots out your transgressions for my own sake, and I will not remember your sins.

Isaiah 43:25

Many libraries offer a grace period on late book returns. They wait a few days before imposing a fine. The "grace period" that Christ offers is entirely different! He paid our fine and has removed the charges. What sins are weighing on your mind? Confess them to the Lord and ask for forgiveness. He stands ready to write "Paid in Full" across your account.

Tangible Grace

Do you have bills to pay today? As you write the checks or pay online, consider how very much more you once owed God. Then rejoice in the fact that Jesus has paid it in full!

Now to him who is able to do far more abundantly than all that we ask or think, according to the power at work within us, to him be glory in the church and in Christ Jesus throughout all generations, forever and ever. Amen.

Ephesians 3:20–21

The eternity that God has planned for you, his forgiven child, will be abundantly more amazing than you could ever imagine. By grace, through faith in Christ, you are given the gift of eternal life with him. That life starts now and extends into all eternity. What are you most looking forward to about heaven?

Tangible Grace

Read your description above and imagine
the joy that it will bring. God's glory and the
future he has planned for you will be better,
thousands of times better!

So that Christ may dwell in your hearts through faith—that you, being rooted and grounded in love, may have strength to comprehend with all the saints what is the breadth and length and height and depth, and to know the love of Christ that surpasses knowledge, that you may be filled with all the fullness of God.

Ephesians 3:17–19

The love of Christ is wider and deeper than we can understand. His love gives you the strength to stay grounded no matter what you are facing. List the issues—big and small—that have you frustrated, worried, or discouraged right now.

Tangible Grace

Go back to the list of issues you wrote above.
Write this truth over each one:
"God's love is bigger!"

I wait for the LORD, my soul waits,
and in his word I hope.

Psalm 130:5

Some difficulties come and then quickly pass. Others come and stay. And stay. Even in those times, though, God's Word brings comfort and hope for the future. Which passages of Scripture fill you with hope?

_____

_____

_____

_____

_____

_____

_____

_____

_____

_____

_____

_____

_____

_____

_____

_____

Tangible Grace

Write one of those verses on an index card and put it in
the pocket of a jacket, skirt, or pair of pants in your
closet. On some future day when you wear that
item of clothing, you will find a reminder of
your hope in Christ!

Come to me, all who labor and are heavy laden, and I will give you rest.

Matthew 11:28

Jesus offers you rest. It comes especially in his forgiveness. You can lay down the burden of guilt. You can stop obsessing over your failed attempts at perfection. The rest Jesus offers doesn't depend on the good that you've done, but on the good that Christ did for you. Which burdens can you bring to him in prayer today?

_____

_____

_____

_____

_____

_____

_____

_____

_____

_____

_____

_____

_____

_____

_____

_____

_____

Tangible Grace

Find three minutes to sit in your favorite chair,
close your eyes, and relax. Thank God for the
rest you find in Christ. Then stand up and smile,
renewed for your next task!

Give ear, O LORD, to my prayer; listen to my plea for grace. In the day of my trouble I call upon you, for you answer me.

Psalm 86:6–7

In his grace, God listens to your prayers and promises to answer you. His answer may not be what you want at the time, but you can trust that he always, always gives you his very best and nothing less. What makes it hard for you to trust that? Ask the Holy Spirit's help in overcoming these obstacles.

Tangible Grace

Hold your phone in your hand.
Whether or not you pick it up each
    time it rings, the Lord always answers
    when you call.

To see all of CTA's devotion books and journals, visit us at www.CTAinc.com. You may order online or by calling 1-800-999-1874.

If this book has made a difference in your life or if you have simply enjoyed it, we would like to hear from you. Your words will encourage us!

E-mail: editor@CTAinc.com; include the subject line: ABG19PJ

Write: Editorial Manager, Department ABG19PJ
CTA, Inc.
PO Box 1205
Fenton, MO 63026-1205

Comment online: www.CTAinc.com
(search ABG19PJ)